STOP SELLING
LET THEM BUY

THE PERSONALITY PLAYBOOK

How to Spot Every Buyer Type, Earn Their Trust,
and Close with Clarity (Not Pressure)

Published by: Staten House

Staten House

STOP SELLING
LET THEM BUY

THE PERSONALITY PLAYBOOK

How to Spot Every Buyer Type, Earn Their Trust,
and Close with Clarity (Not Pressure)

PHILIP VIVIER

Table of Contents

Acknowledgments i

Introduction.. iii

Chapter 1

You're Helping a Personality Buy, Not a Persona......................1

Chapter 2

The Four Buyer Archetypes (and How to Spot Them) 5

Chapter 3

Spotting Their Type in the Wild..12

Chapter 4

Why Features Don't Sell (And What Actually Does) 18

Chapter 5

What Questions Really Do 24

Chapter 6

The Follow-Up That Feels Like a Favor 29

Chapter 7

Stop Aligning — Start Belonging.. 35

Chapter 8

Scripts Kill Trust. Frameworks Build It. 41

Chapter 9

The Question Behind the Question 46

Chapter 10

The Micro-Moments That Make the Sale 51

Chapter 11

When to Walk Away (And Why It Builds Trust)..................... 56

Chapter 12

From Customer to Advocate 61

Chapter 13

Show Up How You'd Want to Be Met 66

Chapter 14

Recap: What Really Builds Trust 70

Acknowledgments

To the buyers who challenged me, ghosted me, questioned me, and taught me more than any sales training ever could — thank you.

To the teams I've led, coached, and learned from — your feedback sharpened these ideas.

To my family — thank you for the unwavering support, belief, and laughter. None of this happens without you.

And to you — the reader who's choosing to lead with empathy instead of ego — I see you. Keep showing up real. The world needs more of that.

Introduction

THIS ISN'T A SALES BOOK (AGAIN)

When I first wrote *Stop Selling – Let Them Buy,* the world was still comfortable with cold calls, scripted demos, and closing lines that sounded like they belonged in a movie, not a meeting. Buyers expected polish. They tolerated pressure. And some even respected the pushy closer.

Then everything changed.

Zoom calls replaced boardroom meetings. Slack replaced hallway conversations. AI began drafting our emails, summarizing our calls, and even writing our follow-ups. We no longer sell in person. We sell in pixels. And with every swipe, scroll, and ignored email, one truth has become clear:

PEOPLE DON'T BUY FROM COMPANIES ANYMORE. THEY BUY FROM PEOPLE.

They buy from people who understand them. Who meet them where they are. Who actually see them — not just as a persona, but as a personality.

And the only way to *really* see someone? Understand who they are before you ever talk about what you're selling.

That was the heartbeat of the first edition. But this one? This goes deeper. This version was built for today's reality — one where attention is scarce, trust is fragile, and buyers can sniff out fake faster than ever.

So, this isn't a book about "how to sell." It's a guide on how to help someone feel safe enough, seen enough, and supported enough to move forward.

LET ME TELL YOU A STORY

A few years back, I had a video call scheduled with a VP of HR at a mid-sized software company. Let's call her Dana. I had done my prep, built my slide deck, and blocked off 45 minutes for what I assumed would be a standard discovery conversation.

We hopped on Zoom, and in the first three minutes, I knew everything needed to shift.

Dana wasn't direct or fast-paced like I expected. She wasn't focused on ROI or deliverables. Instead, she shared how exhausted her team was, how they'd just gone through a restructuring, and how hard it was to keep morale up.

I closed the deck.

Instead, I asked her what kind of support she needed. We talked about culture, burnout, and the human side of change. By the end of the call, she said something that stuck with me: **"You were the first person who didn't try to sell me something today. You just listened. That's why I want to move forward."**

And she did.

What's New in This Edition

If the original *Let Them Buy* gave you the mindset, this edition gives you the map. Not to close harder — but to guide smarter.

You'll learn:

- ☑ How to spot someone's decision-making personality from their Slack replies or LinkedIn DMs

- ☑ How to shape conversations based on how they process information — not just what you want to say

- ☑ How to make your follow-ups feel like favors

- ☑ How AI, Zoom, Teams, and Slack have changed the rhythm of trust — and how to adapt without losing your human touch

This is the field guide to helping people buy — in a world that's faster, more distracted, and more skeptical than ever.

And it all starts with understanding personality.

Not persona. Not industry. Not job title.

Personality.

Because that's what makes the difference between a pitch they tune out and a conversation they lean into.

Let's help people buy.
One personality at a time.

Chapter 1

YOU'RE HELPING A PERSONALITY BUY, NOT A PERSONA

Most sellers are taught to look at personas: job titles, industries, roles, maybe a pain point or two.

That might help with targeting. But it doesn't help with trust.

Because when someone is deciding whether or not to buy, they're not doing it as a job title. They're doing it as a human — with habits, fears, quirks, preferences. With a way they like to process information and a rhythm they use to make decisions.

That's personality. And it drives everything.

When you understand someone's personality, you stop trying to convince them. You start guiding them. Because you know how they need to hear things to feel comfortable moving forward.

You stop trying to close the deal — and instead, you open the path.

This book is about helping people buy in a way that feels safe to them. So they move forward confidently, not cautiously. And they do it faster — not because you pushed, but because you understood.

The Trade Show Misread

Years ago, I was at a conference where dozens of software companies were showcasing new platforms. I'd stopped by a booth that looked interesting — the branding was strong, and the product seemed promising.

Before I could even say hello, a rep walked up and launched into a pitch. Not a conversation. A monologue. Features. Benefits. Demo steps. Then — he paused, looked me up and down, and said:

"You're probably just here to collect swag anyway."

That told me everything I needed to know.

He had slotted me into a box — a persona, not a person. He assumed I wasn't serious. He never asked a question. Never gave me space to speak. Just projected, performed, and passed judgment.

Ironically, I *was* serious. I had a real budget and a real need. But the way he approached me? I was out before he finished his sentence.

That's what happens when you focus on a profile instead of a personality. You miss the chance to connect.

Here's what this chapter — and this book — wants you to walk away with:

You're not dealing with "a VP of Ops at a logistics firm."

You're helping **Dan**, who's a Driver, make a fast decision that won't embarrass him in front of his board.

You're not trying to win over "a marketing director in CPG."

You're guiding **Sandra**, who's a Connector, through a story she'll be proud to tell others when it works.

You're not selling to "a mid-level IT leader at a SaaS company."

You're helping **Thomas**, an Analyst, feel confident that the numbers line up with his logic.

This is the shift.

From pitching a product... to understanding a person.

From checking boxes... to building trust.

From trying to persuade... to helping someone feel ready.

When you stop seeing a buyer as a persona — and start meeting them as a personality — everything changes.

And that's when they buy.

Chapter 2

THE FOUR BUYER ARCHETYPES (AND HOW TO SPOT THEM)

Most people don't buy based on logic alone. They buy based on how something makes them feel — and how well that feeling fits with how they're wired.

What drives one person to move forward might completely stall another. Not because the offer was wrong — but because the approach didn't feel right.

You're not selling to a demographic. You're guiding a personality.

And most personalities fall into one of four dominant buyer types. You'll meet them in nearly every industry, every market, every deal. The more you tune in, the more obvious they become.

Let's break them down.

The Supporter — "Will you take care of me?"

- ☑ **Need:** Safety, connection, support

- ☑ **Fear:** Being pressured or left behind

- ☑ **Buy when:** They trust you and feel confident they'll be cared for after the decision

Supporters are warm, relationship-driven buyers. They don't just want to know *what* you're offering — they want to know *who* you are and how you'll show up once the decision's made.

If a Supporter senses pressure, they shut down. If they feel connection, they open up. They want to feel like you're in it with them — not just until the contract is signed, but long after.

The Driver — "Is this worth my time?"

- ☑ **Need:** Efficiency, clarity, results

- ☑ **Fear:** Wasting time or losing control

- ☑ **Buy when:** The path is fast, direct, and centered on outcomes

Drivers don't linger in conversation. They don't want stories or warm-up talk. They want to know what's next, what it solves, and how fast it works.

They're decisive and focused. But if you're vague, rambling, or indecisive — they'll mentally check out. Not because they're rude, but because their internal meter is always scanning for, "Is this worth it?"

Help them move quickly, and they'll move with you.

The Analyst — "Can I be sure this is right?"

- ☑ **Need:** Accuracy, logic, process

- ☑ **Fear:** Making the wrong decision

- ☑ **Buy when:** The details make sense, and nothing feels rushed

Analysts are deliberate, thorough, and quietly intense. They don't move fast — not because they're unsure of you, but because they need to be sure of everything.

They want proof, precision, and process. They're often the most loyal buyers — but only if they believe your offer can stand up to their scrutiny.

Rush them, and you lose them. Guide them, and they'll follow with confidence.

The Connector — "Does this excite and inspire me?"

- ☑ **Need:** Possibility, energy, momentum

- ☑ **Fear:** Boredom, stagnation, being boxed in

- ☑ **Buy when:** The vision clicks and the relationship sparks

Connectors bring emotion to the table — and expect you to meet them there. They get excited about ideas, momentum, and people who match their energy.

They don't care about technical specs unless they support a story. They want to feel something. To be part of something. To move forward with a "hell yes" — not a cautious maybe.

They buy fast, share often, and stay loyal as long as you keep the vibe alive.

STORY: THE SAME OFFER, FOUR VERY DIFFERENT CONVERSATIONS

A few years back, I was introducing a new service to four different prospective clients in the same week. Same offer. Same pricing. Same benefits.

But the responses? Couldn't have been more different.

Monday's meeting was with a Supporter. A nonprofit director who had clearly done her research. She was polite, patient, and kept circling back to questions about how the process worked *after* she signed on. "What happens if we run into an issue?" "Do we get a dedicated person?" I knew the actual service didn't matter to her until she felt confident in the relationship. So I shifted gears. We talked about how we onboard. How we stay connected. She didn't care about being wowed. She wanted to feel taken care of. We shook hands that afternoon.

Tuesday was a Driver. A regional VP at a logistics firm who barely sat down before saying, "You've got 10 minutes

— what do I need to know?" I went straight to the outcomes. He cut me off halfway through and said, "If it does that, send me what I need to sign. If not, we're done." We were done — in the best way. Contract signed in 24 hours.

Wednesday brought the Analyst. I walked into a conference room and saw charts, notes, and a printout of my website. This buyer had questions — about methodology, tracking, edge cases. It wasn't small talk. It was forensic. I took the time. Explained everything clearly. Followed up with a detailed proposal. They signed three weeks later, after vetting everything. Worth it.

Thursday? The Connector. She greeted me with a hug. I hadn't even met her in person yet. We ended up brainstorming campaign ideas together halfway through our meeting. She barely glanced at the pricing. "This feels good," she said. "I'm in." And she meant it.

WHY THIS MATTERS

When you stop trying to "sell" people and start learning how they buy, everything gets easier.

You stop fighting resistance. You stop over-explaining to someone who needs vision. You stop soft-pedaling with someone who craves directness. You stop handing out logic to someone who's craving trust.

And you start aligning.

Understanding buying personalities isn't about labeling people. It's about liberating them — from feeling pressured, misunderstood, or boxed in.

So take a beat. Listen for clues. Notice their pace, their questions, their tone.

Are they cautious? Curious? Quick-moving? Quiet?

Because once you spot the pattern, you don't need a script.

You just need to speak their language.

And when you do?

They buy — not because you pushed, but because you met them where they are.

chapter 3

SPOTTING THEIR TYPE IN THE WILD

Buyers won't tell you their personality type outright. But they'll show you — in their tone, their pace, their punctuation, even their Slack replies.

This is especially true in today's hybrid and remote world, where most of your sales conversations start not in a boardroom, but in a Zoom call, a Slack DM, or an email thread. Learning to read these cues quickly and accurately is one of the most important trust-building skills you can develop.

Let's break it down:

The Supporter

Supporters write warm, thoughtful messages. They ask how your day is. They open with small talk. You'll notice "hope you're well" in their emails and emojis like ☺ or 🙏 in their Slack messages. They'll tell you they're "looking forward to working together," and they mean it.

On Zoom, they lean in and nod. They're slower to make decisions — not because they're hesitant about the product, but because they care about people. They want to make sure everyone's aligned, comfortable, and cared for.

Your signal: If you get a "Thanks so much for your time today!" Slack message that's longer than two sentences — they're a Supporter.

The Driver

Drivers don't waste time. Their Slack messages are short, sometimes just an emoji (✅). Their emails often skip the greeting entirely and jump right into action: "What's the ETA on this?" or "Need this done by EOD."

In meetings, they're scanning for who's accountable. They want clear next steps and bullet points. They appreciate you respecting their time.

Your signal: If they book a 15-minute Zoom and wrap it up in 10 — you're talking to a Driver.

The Analyst

Analysts bring structure. They write in full sentences, often with bullet points or numbered lists. They ask precise questions and will fact-check what you say. On Slack or Teams, they'll often drop links, attachments, or references to previous threads.

On Zoom, they may appear quiet — but don't mistake that for disinterest. They're evaluating everything.

Your signal: If they share their screen to walk through a spreadsheet — Analyst, 100%.

The Connector

Connectors are expressive and energetic. Their messages are peppered with exclamation points (!!), GIFs, or spontaneous ideas like "What if we...?"

They're the ones who'll send you a voice note on WhatsApp, a Loom instead of a typed response, or fire off a Slack message at midnight because inspiration struck.

Your signal: If their first email includes "This is super exciting!" and ends with a 🎉 — you've got a Connector.

Watch for Clues Across Channels

In today's async-first world, personality cues can show up differently depending on the platform:

- ☑ **Slack:** Watch tone, length, and punctuation. Is it rapid-fire or thoughtful? Formal or casual?

- ☑ **Email:** Are they structured or conversational? Do they include pleasantries or skip them?

- ☑ **Zoom/Teams:** Do they take up space or hang back? Do they ask big-picture questions or drill into details?

The magic is in noticing patterns. One Slack message doesn't define a personality — but a week's worth? That's a goldmine.

Story: The Emoji That Saved a Deal

A few years ago, I was working with a tech startup on a software partnership. Most of the communication was via

Slack. One of the stakeholders — let's call her Kara — would reply with short, emoji-filled messages like "Love this! 🔥" or "YESSSS 😍."

But when I sent a proposal doc, her tone shifted. One-word replies. No emojis. No energy.

Most sellers might've taken that as disinterest and started pushing harder. Instead, I paused. I jumped on Zoom and said, "Hey — I noticed your vibe shifted. Is there something in the proposal that didn't sit right?"

She laughed. "I didn't even realize I was doing that. But yeah — I didn't feel like the package fit us. The pricing tiers felt really rigid."

We reworked it live on the call. She left smiling.

Two hours later: "This is perfect! Thank you!!! 🎉"

That deal could've died in the silence between emojis. But because I paid attention to her rhythm — and noticed when it changed — I was able to catch it.

Don't Mirror. Translate.

Here's the key: you're not trying to mimic their style. You're translating yours into a rhythm they'll receive.

If you're naturally a Driver, you don't need to become warm and fuzzy for a Supporter. But you might slow your pace, soften your tone, and lead with a little more context. It's still you — just tuned to their frequency.

And in today's hybrid world, where personality often comes through in typed words more than spoken ones, your ability to read those signals is a massive differentiator.

Because when someone feels like you get them — even through Slack or Zoom — you've already started building trust.

And that's the first step to letting them buy.

chapter 4

WHY FEATURES DON'T SELL (AND WHAT ACTUALLY DOES)

Most sales conversations still center around features, benefits, and pricing. We get excited about what our product can do, so we talk about it. Endlessly.

We point out the integrations, the dashboards, the customizability. We explain how many widgets, how fast the load time, how intuitive the interface. We demo every button, every toggle, every analytics screen.

And we think, surely now they'll see it.

But features don't close deals. Alignment does.

Here's the truth: people don't buy because they fully understand your product. They buy because they feel like you understand *them*.

They want to feel heard, safe, and supported. They want to feel smart for choosing you. They want to believe that buying from you will solve the *real* problem they have — whether it's clarity, confidence, speed, recognition, or peace of mind.

And that's not in your features. It's in your framing.

WHAT TO LEAD WITH INSTEAD

You lead with what matters *to them*, not what excites *you*. That means putting their personality type first:

- ☑ For a **Supporter**, don't start with "custom dashboards." Start with, "We're with you every step of the way, and we don't disappear after the contract is signed."

- ☑ For a **Driver**, don't talk about the long onboarding. Start with, "Here's how fast you can see ROI."

- ☑ For an **Analyst**, don't skip straight to the outcome. Start with, "Let me show you how the process works, step by step."

☑ For a **Connector**, don't bore them with technical jargon. Start with, "This could unlock something game-changing for your team."

It's not about trickery. It's about translating the product into something personally relevant to *them*.

That's what moves people.

THE REAL REASON PEOPLE BUY

People don't buy products.

They buy relief. They buy momentum. They buy clarity. They buy alignment. They buy identity.

If they're a Supporter, they're buying peace of mind. If they're a Driver, they're buying acceleration. If they're an Analyst, they're buying certainty. If they're a Connector, they're buying inspiration.

Your product might *deliver* those things, but your job is to connect the dots. Not with a pitch. Not with a slide deck. With empathy.

Story: The Time I Bought the Wrong Gym Membership (Almost)

A few years back, I got cold-called by a fitness center. The rep launched right into a script. You could hear the rehearsed rhythm.

"We're currently offering a discount on our personal training packages and prenatal fitness program..."

Wait. Prenatal?

"Excuse me?" I interrupted.

"Yes, for new moms. It's a very popular option right now..."

I paused. "I'm not pregnant."

She paused. Dead air.

Then a rushed apology, some fumbling, and she quickly shifted to talk about something else. But it was too late. The trust was gone.

Not because of the mistake. Mistakes happen. But because it was obvious she wasn't talking to *me*. She was talking *at me*. She wasn't listening. She was pitching. And pitching assumes a one-size-fits-all solution.

She could've asked one question. Just one: "What are your fitness goals right now?"

I would've told her I was recovering from a back injury. Looking for something low-impact. And open to support.

If she had started with me—not her script—she could've had a buyer. Instead, she had a list of features and a lost lead.

Zoom, Slack, AI and the Death of the Pitch

Today, we're not always presenting in person. We're messaging over Teams, replying on Slack, or sending short-form Loom videos.

This means we need to shift from "presentation" to "translation."

Instead of sending the same polished PDF to every prospect, ask ChatGPT to help reframe it for a Connector who needs inspiration. Or for an Analyst who needs steps and documentation. Use AI to shape *your material* around *their mindset.*

It's not just smarter. It's human.

And in an AI-heavy world, the most human seller wins.

So next time you find yourself listing out features, pause. Ask yourself:

☑ What is this person *really* solving for?

☑ What emotion are they buying?

☑ How can I frame this so it feels like a solution *for them*?

When you lead with that, the features still matter. But they become proof, not the pitch.

And buying becomes a no-brainer.

chapter 5

WHAT QUESTIONS REALLY DO

Most people think questions are about getting information.

In sales? They're about creating clarity. Lowering pressure. Giving someone space to think, not forcing them to decide.

When done right, questions do three powerful things:

1. They show respect.

2. They unlock the buyer's own thoughts.

3. They guide, without pushing.

But today, we're asking questions in different environments: Zoom calls, Slack threads, Teams chats, shared docs, even Loom videos. The format might change, but the principle stays the same: smart questions help people buy.

Questions Buyers Actually Want to Answer

Here's how each personality type responds best:

- ☑ **Supporters** respond well to gentle, collaborative language:

  - ◉ "Would it help if we explored that together?"

  - ◉ "What would make this feel like a good decision for your team?"

- ☑ **Drivers** want to move fast and get to the point:

  - ◉ "What's your top priority right now?"

  - ◉ "How do we make this easy to say yes to?"

- ☑ **Analysts** value logic and detail:

  - ◉ "What metrics will you use to evaluate this?"

  - ◉ "Can I walk you through the decision flow we built?"

- ☑ **Connectors** are inspired by vision:

  - ● "What would success look like if we got this right?"

  - ● "How would this free you up to do more of what you love?"

You don't need a script. You just need to listen. Once you hear what matters to them, your next question should point in that direction.

ASKING QUESTIONS ON ZOOM AND SLACK

If you're in a Zoom meeting, you'll often get more truth by asking:

- ☑ "Can I pause here and get your gut reaction?"

- ☑ "Would you be open to riffing on this for a second?"

These loosen the conversation. It stops being a presentation. It becomes a collaboration.

On Slack, short thoughtful questions go a long way:

- ☑ "How's this landing with you so far?"

☑ "Anything here you'd like to change or add?"

You're not interrogating. You're inviting.

STORY: THE SLIDE THAT WASN'T NEEDED

I once had a sales engineer who built a stunning slide deck for a large prospect. Twenty slides. Beautiful graphs. We were ready to present over Zoom.

Right before the meeting, I said, "Let's just see what she asks. If we need the slides, we'll share."

Five minutes in, the buyer — let's call her Sarah — said, "Honestly, I just need to understand one thing: How does this cut our processing time in half without killing our reporting accuracy?"

We never opened the deck.

Instead, we pulled up a shared doc, mapped out the steps, and showed her the logic. Sarah nodded, asked a few clarifiers, and by the end of the call, we were outlining onboarding.

After she signed, she told us, "I felt like you understood how I think. You didn't talk over me. You helped me get clear."

Questions Build the Road — Not the Destination

A good question doesn't need to lead to a "yes." It just needs to lead somewhere valuable — clarity, insight, confidence.

In today's sales environment, people aren't craving better salespeople. They're craving better thinking partners.

So instead of trying to steer someone toward a close, ask the kind of questions that help them steer themselves.

Let them lead — and you'll be surprised how often they choose your path.

Chapter 6

THE FOLLOW-UP THAT FEELS LIKE A FAVOR

Most follow-ups feel awkward — like knocking on a door that someone already closed. Why? Because too often, they're rooted in pressure, not partnership.

But when done right, a follow-up doesn't feel like a nudge. It feels like a favor — a gentle reminder that the door is still open, that you haven't forgotten them, and that you're still here when they're ready.

The key? Tailor your follow-up to how *they* process decisions — and that means knowing their buying personality.

The Supporter

What they need: Reassurance and connection

Follow-up strategy:

- ☑ Use a warm, friendly, non-pushy tone

- ☑ Reinforce that you're here when they're ready

- ☑ Share a brief story or testimonial that builds trust

Example:

"Just wanted to check in and see how everything's feeling on your end. No pressure at all — I'm here if anything bubbles up. Thought I'd share a quick note from another client who felt the same way early on... they're loving the results now."

The Driver

What they need: Brevity and control

Follow-up strategy:

- ☑ Get to the point — fast

- ☑ Offer a clear next step

- ☑ Remind them of the payoff

Example:

"For clarification — I can have your setup finalized by Friday if we get the green light this week. Takes less than 10 minutes to launch. Want me to send the link?"

The Analyst

What they need: Clarity and logic

Follow-up strategy:

- ☑ Summarize key points in structured bullets
- ☑ Include a resource, report, or framework
- ☑ Invite them to explore deeper if helpful

Example:

"As promised, here's a one-page summary of everything we discussed, with answers to the questions you raised. Let me know if you'd like to walk through the numbers together. Happy to schedule a 15-minute breakdown."

The Connector

What they need: Energy and vision

Follow-up strategy:

- ☑ Keep the tone upbeat and personal

- ☑ Tie back to their bigger picture

- ☑ Remind them that the momentum is still there

Example:

"Hey! Still thinking about that idea you shared on the call — honestly, it's stuck with me. When you're ready to bring it to life, I'm all in. This is going to be fun."

A STORY: THE FOLLOW-UP THAT LANDED THE DEAL

Years ago, I had a prospect named Jenna who had gone quiet after a promising call. Most salespeople would've assumed she wasn't interested. But I remembered how she spoke — warm, thoughtful, and deeply loyal to her team. A Supporter, no question.

So instead of a hard nudge, I sent her this:

"Hey Jenna — just checking in to see how everything's feeling. I know decisions like this aren't made lightly, especially when you care so much about your people. I'm here if anything feels unclear or unfinished."

She responded 15 minutes later:

"Thank you for this. Honestly, I've been torn because I wanted to be sure we'd be taken care of. This helped. Can we chat tomorrow?"

That call turned into a signed agreement. But more importantly, it turned into trust.

TECH-SAVVY TOUCHPOINTS

The world we follow up in has changed. It's not just about emails and voicemails anymore.

- ☑ Slack/Teams: Drop a short DM that matches their tone. A Driver might get "Still good for Thursday's rollout?" while a Connector gets "This week's going to be 🔥 — ready to roll?"

- ☑ Zoom or Video Looms: Record a 1-minute personalized check-in. An Analyst will love a screen share with updated data. A Supporter will appreciate seeing your face and hearing your tone.

☑ AI-powered tools: Use AI to help track engagement — but don't let it automate your empathy. A tool can tell you when someone opened your proposal. Only you can follow up with emotional intelligence.

FINAL THOUGHT

A great follow-up doesn't chase. It reopens the conversation with empathy, insight, and respect.

You're not just reminding them — you're reminding *why* they felt seen in the first place.

And when it's framed like a favor — not a follow-up — people don't lean out. They lean in.

Let them buy — when they're ready, because you stayed ready.

Chapter 7

STOP ALIGNING – START BELONGING

L et's get something straight — I despise the word "pitch." It immediately sets up a power imbalance. In baseball, the pitcher isn't working *with* you — they're throwing something *at* you, trying to strike you out. The batter's job is to resist, to swing, to survive.

And yet, that's how many sales professionals are still trained to approach conversations. As if the buyer is the opponent. As if your job is to throw them something slick and hope they hit.

But this book isn't about getting people to swing. It's about making them feel safe enough to step up to the plate in the first place.

The truth is: buyers don't want to be pitched. They want to feel aligned. Even more than that — they want to feel like they *belong* in the solution you're offering.

So let's shift the model. From convincing... to co-creating. From "I'll show you what we do" to "Let's figure out what works for you."

PERSONALITY-DRIVEN ALIGNMENT

Here's what alignment looks like through the lens of buyer personality types:

Supporters

- ☑ Focus on shared values and partnership.

- ☑ Ask: "How can I support your team in a way that feels seamless?"

- ☑ Avoid urgency language. Instead, offer calm, thoughtful next steps.

Drivers

- ☑ Respect their time and decision-making speed.

- ☑ Lead with outcomes, timelines, and ROI.

- ☑ Ask: "Do you want me to summarize what we can deliver by end of quarter?"

Analysts

- ☑ Be clear, structured, and logic-led.

- ☑ Offer frameworks, breakdowns, and rationale.

- ☑ Ask: "Would you like me to send a comparison grid or deeper analysis?"

Connectors

- ☑ Spark imagination.

- ☑ Anchor the conversation in possibilities, growth, and vision.

- ☑ Ask: "Where do you see this taking your team in 6 months if we nailed it?"

This is less about performance and more about presence. If you're truly tuned into *how* someone buys, you'll naturally find the rhythm that lets them move forward without friction.

WHERE THE "PITCH" FAILS — A STORY

A while back, I was CC'd on an outreach email from a rep on our team. They had been trying to land a big opportunity with a tech startup — one we really wanted.

The buyer — a sharp, high-energy VP of Product — had seemed interested on the first call. But since then, silence. So the rep sent over a follow-up message.

It was templated. Full of buzzwords. "Let's jump on a quick call to walk you through our value prop and show you how we're different."

Predictably, no reply.

I suggested we change it up. Instead of another push, we sent a video message — under 60 seconds — recorded in Slack using a webcam:

"Hey John, hope your week's going well. Totally understand if now's not the right time — just wanted to check if anything felt off about what we shared. We're happy to rework things, or hit pause. Either way, we're rooting for you and here if it helps."

That same afternoon, the VP replied:

"Appreciate the human approach. Honestly, I'm drowning in decisions right now. But this made me want to take another look."

They booked a call. And they bought — not because of a better pitch, but because we stopped pitching.

We made space. We made it safe. We made it *belonging*.

ALIGNING IN A VIRTUAL WORLD

AI and automation are everywhere. Slack threads never stop. Zoom fatigue is real. The modern buyer's attention span is split across screens and tasks.

So how do you align when the channel is digital?

- ☑ **In Slack or Teams:** Mirror their tone. If they're concise, be concise. If they use emojis or casual sign-offs, don't go overly formal. Speak their rhythm.

- ☑ **On Zoom:** Keep your screen presence tight. Use visuals that match their style — charts for Analysts, roadmaps for Drivers, inspirational snapshots for Connectors.

- ☑ **Using AI tools:** Use AI to prep smarter, not fake harder. Draft emails that respect their time. Surface insights that matter to *them*, not just what's easy to generate.

Alignment today means fluidity. It's not just about what you say, but *how*, *where*, and *when* you say it.

FINAL THOUGHT: BELONGING OVER PITCHING

When a buyer feels like the solution was *built for them*, resistance melts away.

They don't feel sold to. They feel understood.

And that's the real magic — not in closing the deal, but in opening the door.

Let them buy — not because you pushed, but because you partnered.

That's alignment. That's belonging. That's how modern buyers say yes.

Chapter 8

SCRIPTS KILL TRUST. FRAMEWORKS BUILD IT.

Let's be honest — you can smell a script from a mile away. So can your buyers.

We've all been on the receiving end of a cold call or email that sounded robotic, generic, or just plain off. And what do we do the moment we sense it? We tune out. We push back. We hang up.

Why? Because scripts signal that the other person isn't *really* listening — they're performing.

Frameworks, on the other hand, are flexible. They give you a structure but leave room for real conversation.

A framework lets you:

- ☑ Stay focused, but not rigid

- ☑ Personalize based on personality type

- ☑ Adapt in the moment based on tone, mood, or situation

THE "TECH BRO" EMAIL THAT BACKFIRED

A few months ago, a friend of mine — we'll call her Rachel — received an outreach email from a SaaS company. On the surface, it looked well-crafted: bold subject line, high-energy language, and a clear CTA.

But then she opened it.

It read like someone had taken a ChatGPT prompt and never edited it. It opened with:

"Hi there! As a fellow fast-scaling business, I know how hard it is to manage your SDR pipeline while still prioritizing top-of-funnel velocity..."

Rachel runs a nonprofit dog rescue.

She's not in tech. She doesn't have an SDR team. And she had never once referred to her work as "scaling fast" — she'd actually just been looking for help automating volunteer scheduling.

It was clear the rep had just plugged her into a template designed for startup execs and fired it off without a second glance.

The worst part? They followed up three more times with the exact same wording — just slightly reshuffled.

Rachel's response?

"I'm sure your service helps someone. But I'm not someone. Please remove me from your list."

No reply. Just silence.

That's the danger of scripting at scale. You might think you're reaching more people — but you're not really reaching anyone. Because if it doesn't *feel* personal, it might as well be spam.

That's the risk of a script. It assumes instead of listens. It talks *at* instead of *with*.

Let's take a look at how this plays out across personality types.

The Supporter

What backfires: Aggressive language or high-pressure tactics. **What works:** A warm, reassuring tone that invites dialogue. Replace "I need a decision today" with "Take the time you need — I'm here when you're ready."

The Driver

What backfires: Over-explaining or rambling. **What works:** Clear, confident communication. Give them a bullet-point breakdown of value and the fastest way to act.

The Analyst

What backfires: Fluff, hype, or ambiguity. **What works:** Data-backed responses. Show your reasoning. Be precise. "Based on what you told me, this option gives you a 27% higher ROI."

The Connector

What backfires: Dry, impersonal interactions. **What works:** Emotional resonance and a conversational tone. "Your idea yesterday really stuck with me — I'd love to explore how that ties into this solution."

Scripts belong in theater. Conversations belong in sales.

Frameworks give you a reliable way to stay grounded in purpose, while giving your personality room to show up. They let you flex. They let you connect.

And most importantly — they help you earn trust.

Because no one ever said, "Wow, I really loved being sold to by that human teleprompter."

chapter 9

THE QUESTION BEHIND THE QUESTION

When a buyer asks a question, it's almost never just about the words they use.

"Can you send me more info?" might actually mean, *I don't trust you yet.*

"Is there a discount?" might mean, *I'm not sure the value is clear.*

"Do you offer this in blue?" could really mean, *I need to feel like this reflects me.*

Behind every question is a *story*, a *concern*, or a *desire* that's often unspoken — but deeply real.

The best salespeople don't just answer what's asked. They pause. They dig. And they respond to the question *beneath* the question.

THE SOFTWARE DEMO THAT WASN'T ABOUT SOFTWARE

I once sat in on a call with a sales rep from a tech company. The buyer — a CFO — kept asking highly specific questions about API compatibility, response time, and audit logs.

The rep answered everything perfectly... on paper. But the CFO never engaged. Eventually, the deal stalled.

When I followed up with the CFO privately, he admitted: "Honestly, I just wanted to know if they've done this before — with a company like ours. It's not the tech I doubt. It's whether they understand how complex we are."

He never said that out loud. But every question he asked was *pointing to it*.

And that's what this chapter is about.

Let's look at what kinds of *hidden questions* show up behind the surface ones — and how to listen between the lines.

The Supporter

What they say:

"Is there someone I can talk to if I have questions later?"

What they really mean:

Will I be supported — or left hanging after I buy?

What to listen for:

Their need for reassurance. Don't just say "yes" — paint a picture of what that support looks like: "You'll have a dedicated contact. Here's what that first week would look like with us..."

The Driver

What they say:

"What kind of results have other companies seen?"

What they really mean:

Is this worth my time? Will this make me look smart?

What to listen for:

Their focus on outcomes. Keep your answer short, clear, and confident. "Here's the ROI we've delivered for clients like you — in under 30 days."

The Analyst

What they say:

"What's your process for implementation?"

What they really mean:

Is this going to break something? Have you thought this through?

What to listen for:

Their need for control. Offer a step-by-step, and leave room for them to ask detailed follow-ups without feeling rushed.

The Connector

What they say:

"Do you have any case studies or stories?"

What they really mean:

Can I see myself in this? Does this feel right?

What to listen for:

Their emotional antenna. Stories, testimonials, and even metaphors can be more persuasive than data here.

The question they ask is just the tip of the iceberg. Your job is to *see what's underneath* — and respond like someone who gets it.

Because when people feel heard at that level, the conversation changes.

They're no longer just evaluating a product. They're experiencing *being understood*.

And that? That's what earns the yes.

Chapter 10

THE MICRO-MOMENTS THAT MAKE THE SALE

Sales don't live and die in boardrooms. They're not decided in your pitch deck or your pricing proposal.

They're won (or lost) in the micro-moments:

- ☑ How fast you replied to their email.

- ☑ Whether your tone matched theirs.

- ☑ If your follow-up respected their time.

- ☑ Whether it felt like you were helping... or hurrying them.

Let me give you a real example.

The Five-Minute Window

A client of mine — a senior leader at a large healthcare network — told me a story about how she chose a vendor for a major software overhaul. She had reached out to two companies. Both had similar products, similar pricing, and solid reputations.

But only one replied to her initial email within five minutes — with a short, direct, warm response: "Got your message — yes, we can help. I'll send you a few times for tomorrow, and if it's easier to just hop on now, I've got the next 20 minutes open."

She took the call.

What stood out wasn't just the speed — it was the tone. It wasn't frantic. It wasn't pushy. It was present. That moment set the tone for the entire relationship.

She never replied to the second vendor.

These micro-moments are where trust is built.

Let's break down what those look like for each type.

The Supporter

Micro-moment that matters: When they ask a small question and you take it seriously.

What to do:

Don't rush. A warm, patient reply makes them feel valued. Even if it's a "silly" question to you, it's not to them.

Why it works: Supporters buy when they feel seen and safe. These little acts reinforce that.

The Driver

Micro-moment that matters: When they ask for a next step and you deliver — fast.

What to do:

Don't make them chase you. Respond quickly with one simple action they can take. Bonus points if it saves them time.

Why it works: Drivers equate speed with competence. You either keep up... or you're out.

The Analyst

Micro-moment that matters: When they raise a concern and you calmly offer data.

What to do:

Avoid defensiveness. Thank them for the question, and send a helpful chart, link, or reference. Follow it with an open-ended invite: "Want to dig into this together?"

Why it works: Analysts don't want hype. They want clarity. Show them you're prepared.

The Connector

Micro-moment that matters: When they mention an idea, and you remember it later.

What to do:

Bring it up on the next call. "I was thinking about what you said the other day — that stuck with me."

Why it works: Connectors thrive on personal connection. Remembering what matters to them makes you magnetic.

These small interactions are the real sales engine.

You don't have to nail all of them. But the more consistent you are in showing up as thoughtful, responsive, and human — the more buyers feel like they're already in good hands.

Because people don't buy from processes. They buy from people.

And it's the micro-moments that prove what kind of person you are.

chapter 11

WHEN TO WALK AWAY (AND WHY IT BUILDS TRUST)

Not every buyer is your buyer. Not every opportunity is meant to close. And sometimes, the most trust-building move you can make... is stepping back.

It's counterintuitive, especially in sales cultures built on quotas and urgency. But walking away — with grace and sincerity — often leaves the door wider open than pushing ever could.

Why? Because when you walk away for the *right* reasons, you prove you're not just in it for the win. You're in it for the fit.

THE DEAL I DIDN'T CHASE

Years ago, I was working with a prospect who seemed like a great fit on paper — the right industry, the right budget, even the right pain points.

But something felt off.

Every call was rescheduled. Every question I asked was met with vague answers. Every time I tried to clarify what they really needed, the conversation turned into, "Just send me pricing."

So I did something I rarely did back then.

I said, "Hey, I want to be respectful of your time and mine — and it feels like you might not be sure this is what you need right now. No pressure either way. If it's a no, that's totally fine."

There was a pause. Then he actually sighed in relief.

"You're right," he said. "We're being pushed by our board to look at solutions, but we're not ready to implement anything. I appreciate you saying that."

We stayed in touch. Six months later, he came back — ready, clear, and grateful. And we moved forward fast.

WHAT WALKING AWAY SOUNDS LIKE

- ☑ "This might not be the right time — and that's okay."

- ☑ "I don't want to push this forward if you're unsure."

- ☑ "I'd rather pause here than pressure you into something that doesn't feel right."

These aren't signs of weakness. They're signs of maturity. And in a world full of aggressive closes, this kind of honesty stands out.

Let's look at how each personality responds when *you* are the one who pauses or pulls back:

The Supporter

How they feel: Relieved.

Why: They were likely afraid to say no or didn't want to disappoint you.

What to do: Reassure them the relationship matters more than the deal. Keep the connection warm.

The Driver

How they feel: Respectful.

Why: You didn't waste their time — and you showed clarity and control.

What to do: Stay direct. Let them know you're here when the need becomes real.

The Analyst

How they feel: Validated.

Why: They appreciate someone who recognizes timing and logic over pressure.

What to do: Leave the door open with data they can return to. Keep it factual, not emotional.

The Connector

How they feel: Intrigued.

Why: Your honesty broke the usual script. You weren't trying to win — you were being real.

What to do: Leave them with a story, a possibility, or a vision they can return to when the time feels right.

Sometimes, walking away is the very move that brings them back.

Not today. Maybe not tomorrow. But when the timing is right, they'll remember how you made them feel:

- ☑ Respected

- ☑ Understood

- ☑ Unpressured

And that's when they'll reach out — not because you chased them, but because you didn't.

chapter 12

FROM CUSTOMER TO ADVOCATE

The best sales strategy isn't just about closing deals — it's about opening relationships.

Let me tell you about Sarah.

Sarah was a small business owner I had worked with early in my career. She was hesitant at first — skeptical, cautious, and brutally honest. It wasn't an easy win. I had to meet her where she was, adjust my style to match hers (she was definitely an Analyst-Driver blend), and prove over time that I wasn't there to pressure — I was there to assist.

We eventually closed the deal. But the magic happened after the sale.

Because I didn't disappear.

I checked in. I answered questions she didn't even know to ask. I sent her a note when I saw her brand featured in a local magazine. And months later, when she got a big client win using the platform we'd implemented, I sent her a gift card with a handwritten note: " That's what winning looks like!"

Sarah became one of our biggest champions. She referred over a dozen clients in the next two years — and I never once asked her to.

She *wanted* to.

What happens after the sale is where loyalty is earned, advocacy is created, and growth becomes exponential. And just like everything else in this book, the way you nurture that relationship should flex to who they are.

When someone buys from you, that's the beginning. Not the finish line.

Because not all customers stay engaged the same way. Some need reassurance. Others want updates. Some want a spotlight. Others prefer a quiet check-in.

Let's break it down.

The Supporter

What they need post-sale: Consistent, caring follow-up.

How to turn them into advocates:

Make them feel like part of the family. Share updates. Celebrate their wins. Ask how it's going without an agenda. They'll refer others when they know you'll treat them with the same care.

The Driver

What they need post-sale: Results and recognition.

How to turn them into advocates:

Follow up with ROI data. Highlight how their decision created impact. Offer insider access or early previews — something that reinforces they made a smart move.

The Analyst

What they need post-sale: Transparency and clarity.

How to turn them into advocates:

Keep them in the loop with progress reports, product updates, and detailed resources. Invite them to offer feedback — they'll value the structure and contribute meaningfully.

The Connector

What they need post-sale: Engagement and expression.

How to turn them into advocates:

Spotlight them. Feature their story (with permission). Ask for creative input. Give them something they can share — they'll love the chance to be part of something bigger.

Turning a buyer into an advocate isn't about asking for referrals.

It's about earning their trust so deeply, they want to tell others — not because you asked, but because they're proud to be part of what you're building.

They become an extension of your brand. A signal to others that you're the real deal.

Because when you stop selling and start aligning, people don't just buy from you.

They believe in you.

chapter 13

SHOW UP HOW YOU'D WANT TO BE MET

If everything in this book could be summed up in one principle, it's this:

THE HOME VISIT

Years ago, I visited a client onsite for what was supposed to be a typical review meeting. But when I got there, things felt off. The client — a normally energetic and decisive COO — was distracted, tense, and unusually quiet.

I paused the agenda and asked, "Is everything alright? We can reschedule if now's not a good time."

She hesitated, then told me her teenage son had just been suspended from school and she'd spent the morning in meetings with the principal.

"I'm sorry," I said. "Honestly, this meeting can wait. Let's just have coffee. You don't need a vendor today — you need a breather."

We sat and talked for 30 minutes. Not about business. Not about goals. Just life.

She later told me that moment solidified our relationship. She went from client to advocate, not because of a discount, pitch, or clever follow-up — but because I treated her like a human first.

Show up how you'd want someone to show up for you.

Not how the playbook says. Not how your CRM nudges you. Not how the guru in your feed pitches it. But how *you* would want someone to show up if you were on the other side.

Because no one wants to feel hunted. No one wants to be pushed. And no one wakes up hoping to be "closed."

But we *do* want to be understood. We want to feel like our time matters. We want to feel like the person on the other end isn't just trying to win — they're trying to help.

This is what trust looks like in action. It means letting go of tired sales tactics and instead:

- ☑ Reading people better

- ☑ Listening deeper

- ☑ Matching your style to theirs

- ☑ And most of all — showing up like a real person

You're not pushing. You're aligning. You're helping someone make a decision they can feel great about.

And ironically? That's what makes them buy.

I used to chase every deal. Script every line. Try to "pitch" my way through objections. And I was good at it — but I was also exhausted.

It wasn't until I started focusing on trust over technique, and people over pressure, that everything changed. Deals got easier. Referrals started coming. And conversations felt lighter — because I wasn't performing anymore.

So here's my final ask to you: Before your next call, meeting, email, or proposal... pause.

Ask yourself:

If I were them, how would I want to be approached? Spoken to? Helped?

Then do that.

That's not just how you show up. That's how you build something that lasts.

Because at the end of the day, the goal isn't to sell. **It's to let them buy**

Chapter 14

RECAP: WHAT REALLY BUILDS TRUST

If you remember nothing else from this book, remember this:

- ☑ Buyers are people, not personas.

- ☑ Trust is built in how you show up, not what you sell.

- ☑ Frameworks > scripts. Connection > pitch.

- ☑ Personality matters — yours and theirs.

- ☑ When in doubt, ask yourself: *How would I want to be treated right now?*

Because when people feel understood, they let their guard down. And when that happens — they buy.

Let them.

www.ingramcontent.com/pod-product-compliance
Lightning Source LLC
Chambersburg PA
CBHW051643120626
46551CB00015B/2200